101 440 663 3

D1465172

The Power of Added Value

LEARNING CENTRE
WITHDRAWN FROM STOCK

ONE WEEK LOAN

1 1 MAR 2003

1 0 JAN 1997

3 0 JAN 1995

6-2-95
16/2/95 .

12 NOV 1999

2 3 FEB 1998

2 8 FEB 1996

1 8 FEB 1999

2 4 NOV 1999

1 3 DEC 1999

2 4 MAY 1999

1 3 MAR 1996

2 4 JAN 2000

21 OCT 1999

2 2 MAY 1996

0 5 APR 2000

2 9 OCT 1999

17/4/00

2 7 SEP 1996

3 0 MAY 2001   1 4 FEB 2002

- 9 MAR 1998

3 0 JAN 2003

2 3 NOV 2000

© The material in this text is the copyright of The authors and the intellectual property of David Chapman.

The value added performance charts are the copyright of David J. Chapman and John N. Boyce (1981)

ISBN 0-9522008-0-5

Published by Eaglehead Publishing Limited,
The Old Forge, Barnsley Park,
Barnsley, Cirencester,
Gloucestershire
GL7 5EG

SHEFFIELD HALLAM UNIVERSITY LIBRARY
WL
658·802
CH
TOTLEY

Data Conversion, Printed and Bound by Bourne Press Limited, Bournemouth.

Foreword

The economic recession from which industry is now slowly emerging has been particularly difficult for the printing industry. Nevertheless, companies who have continued to focus on the customer have survived and in some cases managed to grow, both in physical terms and in profit terms. However, in spite of a slowly improving economic climate the commercial pressures on printers will not abate. This is due to technological substitution, overseas competition and increasing capacity due to improved manufacturing techniques. Maintaining a competitive edge is therefore going to be vitally important.

The authors of this work have collaborated previously in the production of two publications, where the research confirmed that successful companies in the industry had effective marketing and pricing policies and focused on the management of value added rather than revenue. This text, which is based on extensive consultancy work in the printing industry, takes the reader further than just exhortation. It demonstrates how the analysis of products and markets can give managers high grade information on which to target markets and price effectively. In other words it gives the information on how to match the opportunities and threats in the market place with the strengths and weaknesses of the firm, and to harness the power of value added in the development and implementation of good marketing plans.

Nick Hutton,
Managing Director, Greenup and Thompson Ltd.,
Sheffield
President BPIF, 1993

Dedication

For John and Anthea Chapman and Liz Hill

CONTENTS

INTRODUCTION

CHAPTER 1

VALUE ADDED AND CONTRIBUTION ANALYSIS OF MANAGEMENT ACCOUNTS

CHAPTER 2

MARKET SEGMENTATION

CHAPTER 3

VALUE ADDED AND CONTRIBUTION ANALYSIS OF JOB SHEETS

CHAPTER 4

CONTRIBUTION CONTOUR GRID ANALYSIS OF PRODUCTS AND MARKETS

CHAPTER 5

DEVELOPING A MARKETING STRATEGY

CHAPTER 6

USING PRICE TO SUPPORT A MARKETING STRATEGY

CHAPTER 7

DEVELOPING A BUSINESS PLAN

ILLUSTRATIONS

APPENDIX

INTRODUCTION

The aim of this book is to help managers improve their company's performance and bottom line profits by making the best use of their management information systems. The companies which succeed these days are those which have good information systems that link up information on how they are performing in the market place with information on their costs of production enabling them to take decisions which will help to maximise profits. The book will provide managers with the analytical tools and the methodology to use their management information systems to generate profits.

Research carried out by the authors in the printing industry, reinforced by consultancy in numerous printing firms over the last fifteen years, has shown that successful firms have:

• clear corporate objectives;

• a well defined marketing strategy;

• a clear understanding of money and its use as a company resource;

• good decision making procedures based on good information systems;

• managers who work well as a team and are well trained to meet the changing needs of the business.

The more successful firms are those which concentrate on generating revenue and increasing value added while containing costs. The less successful firms concentrate only on managing costs. This has particularly been the case during times of economic recession. Revenue generation is about bringing more money into the business through increasing volume sales and/or raising prices. Value added analysis and market segmentation backed up by market pricing are a means of targeting sales to achieve this. All of which requires good information systems relating the prices being obtained in the market place to the costs of production in the factory so that management knows which markets are generating the best value added and which it should be targeting with which products.

It might appear difficult to achieve increased sales and higher prices in highly competitive and constrained markets, but that is what the more successful firms have achieved by targeting their sales into those markets where the value added per £ of sales and per £ of wages is highest and away from markets yielding low value added per £ of sales and wages. They have found ways of adding value to their products as a means of generating more revenue per unit of output and input. These "hidden" price increases resulting from better directed sales effort have been much more effective in improving profitability than cost cutting exercises which have simply l eft resources stretched and unable to cope with any extra business.

The book explains how to develop a business plan and marketing strategy aimed at revenue generation and based on market segmentation and market pricing. To do this efficiently a firm needs to have good information about markets and about its own position in them. It also needs to have good information about the value added which the products it is selling into those markets are generating.

The book describes the management information that is required, where it can be found within the organisation, how to use it to develop a business plan and marketing strategy and how to make pricing decisions and target markets in support of the strategy. It also introduces and explains the management tools needed to analyse and make use of the information.

The management tools in question are:

• value added and contribution analysis - for analysing management accounts and calculating the worth of work for different products and markets;

• market segmentation - for analysing sales in terms of products and markets;

• market targeting - for developing marketing strategies to optimise profits using pricing policies which differentiate between markets;

• market based pricing - for pricing products for different markets on the basis of value added and contribution analysis; and

• business planning - for developing a business plan to generate a required level of sales, value added and profits.

CHAPTER 1

VALUE ADDED AND CONTRIBUTION AND THE ANALYSIS OF MANAGEMENT ACCOUNTS

What is value added?

1.01 The value added which a firm derives from selling its products is the sales value of those products less the purchase price of the raw materials and outwork which the firm had to buy in order to produce them. In other words it is the value which, in the eyes of the customers, the firm adds to those materials and bought in outwork in the production of saleable goods. A printer, for example, buys in paper and perhaps some typesetting and binding and produces a book. The value added is the difference between what the publisher pays for the book and the cost to the printer of the paper and the typesetting and binding outwork.

1.02 The value added produced by an organisation is work done (sales adjusted for work in progress) less productive materials used. Value added, therefore, is influenced by the sales activity of the company through volume, price and mix of work and through the management of materials usage and outwork. For example, a change towards an expensive paper could have a significant effect on materials usage and a sales value increase might hide a fall off in value added. The use of this measure therefore compensates for different materials usage, and value added rather than sales is a true measure of the commercial progress and performance of a company. Furthermore, because printers produce such a diverse mix of work with different materials content, measuring value added is a major first step in the introduction of an effective pricing policy.

Illustration 1 The value added cake

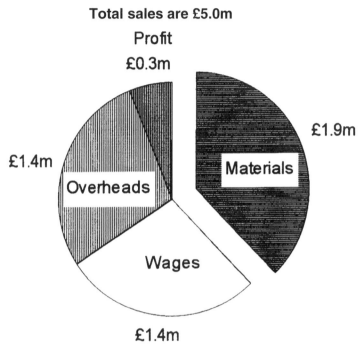

Total sales are £5.0m

Profit
£0.3m

£1.9m

£1.4m

Materials

Overheads

Wages

£1.4m

1.03 The amount of value added created is also important because out of it the firm pays wages and salaries to its employees, overheads to various providers of services, interest to banks, taxes to the government and dividends to its shareholders, hopefully having something left over to plough back into the business as retained earnings.

Contribution and net profit

1.04 The second important measure is that of contribution, which is the value added less the direct wages paid in a company. Value added and contribution are directly influenced by the effectiveness of the management of the company and give true figures of resource costs. They take out any masking of apportionment of overheads.

The use of contribution analysis is often cited as a good business measure, but its sole use can have disadvantages as will be shown later. Together value added and contribution can be used to calculate some important performance measures.

1.05 Contribution is what is left after direct production wages have been paid out of value added. It goes towards meeting overheads and net profits. Net profit is what is left after overheads have been deducted from contribution.

The use of value added and contribution analysis

1.06 Value added and contribution analysis is the means by which we examine the overall performance of a firm and also identify which products and markets bring in the best returns. The analysis requires inputs from the firm's information system at two levels - at the level of the management accounts and the level of the individual job cost sheet. The management account route leads towards the business plan via overall year end performance ratios, while the job cost sheet route leads towards the marketing strategy and market pricing via the same performance ratios calculated for individual jobs and product/market cells, and the identification of those products and markets which provide the best returns. The two routes meet on a contribution contour grid.

1.07 A simple value added and contribution statement can be drawn up from a firm's management accounts as follows:

Illustration 2 Value added and contribution analysis of management accounts

	£'000s
Sales	5000
less materials	1500
less outwork	400
= Value Added	3100
less direct wages	1400
= Contribution	1700
less overheads	1400
= Net Profit	300

1.08 A more detailed statement showing how the various items in the management accounts would be allocated is shown at appendix A . The statement is for the most recent year and will be the basis on which the business plan for future years is constructed. The figure for sales should be less discounts and any quantity rebates and adjusted for stocks. The figure for purchases should include materials, outwork, agents' commission and payments for outside transport all of which should be shown separately. The figure for wages should be for direct production employees and should include all wages paid including overtime, holiday pay, bonuses and employers' contributions to National Insurance and any company pension scheme. Overheads should include administration salaries and other items normally included within overheads. It is useful to calculate profits before depreciation, interest and tax and then to show depreciation, leasing and interest separately before deducting them to arrive at the bottom line of profits before tax.

Break even chart

1.09 Value added and contribution can also be graphically expressed on a break even chart, see illustration 3. The vertical axis measures the value of sales and purchases while the horizontal axis measures the volume of output/ level of utilisation. For the purposes of translating annual management accounts onto the chart it is convenient to plot "output/utilisation" for the year at 100%, although in reality actual utilisation, as will be seen later, will not have been at that level.

Illustration 3 Break even chart

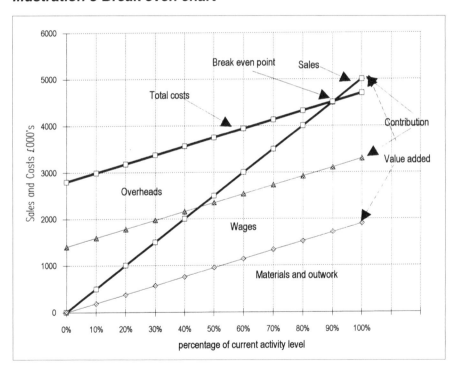

1.10 The sales line is plotted from zero to £5,000,000 against the vertical axis and at 100% along the horizontal axis. The purchases of materials and outwork, which are a variable cost and a function of the level of sales, are then plotted with a line from zero to £1,900,000 against the vertical axis and 100% along the horizontal axis. The area between the sales line and the purchases line represents value added, which at for the year end at "100% utilisation" is £3,100,000.

1.11 Direct wages are regarded as a fixed cost, incurred whatever the level of sales during the year, and are plotted with a line parallel to that for purchases starting at £1,400,000 and continuing to £3,300,000 (i.e. £1,400,000 above £1,900,000 at 100% utilisation along the horizontal axis). Overheads are also a fixed cost and therefore plotted with a line parallel to the wages line and starting a further £1,400,000 above it on the vertical axis and finishing at £4,700,000 at 100% utilisation. The area between the sales line and the overheads line represents net profit which only becomes positive once the sales line has crossed above the line combining purchases, wages and overheads, i.e. at the break even point. Above that point any value added that is generated goes straight into net profit.

1.12 The value of using the break even chart is that it shows clearly the impact of an increase in sales and or prices on the amount of value added and net profit generated. An increase of 5% in volume sales at the same overall average unit price would mean that the sales line would continue on to £5,250,000 along the vertical axis and 105% along the horizontal axis. The purchases of materials and outwork line, being a function of the volume of sales, would also continue forward to 105% on the horizontal axis rising to £1, 995,000 on the vertical axis. But there would be no increase in wages or overheads because they are in this instance regarded as fixed costs. The assumption being made is that the extra volume of output could be achieved without employing more labour or working overtime and without incurring additional overheads. The effect is even more marked with a 10% increase in sales as the chart shows.

Illustration 4 Impact of a 5% increase in volume sales

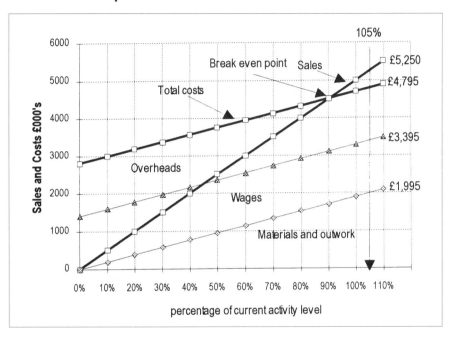

1.13 An increase of 5% in prices would result in an increase in sales value of 5% at the same level of volume sales and hence utilisation. The sales line would rise more steeply meeting the 100% utilisation line at £5,250,000 on the vertical axis. With no increase in purchases of materials or outwork, because volume sales have not increased, and with no increase in wages and overheads, the effect would be to reach the break even point at a lower level of output and an increase in value added and net profits equal to the full increase in sales value i.e. £250,000.

1.14 In contrast a cost cutting exercise which reduced the wages or overheads bill by 5% from £1,400,000 to £1,330,000 while maintaining utilisation at 100% and sales at £5,000,000 would not result in any increase in value added and would produce an increase of only £70,000 in net profit. This is shown in illustration 6 overleaf.

1.15 The importance of pursuing the generation of value added will be clear from these three examples. Expressed in terms of net profit/sales the results of the three alternatives are shown in illustration 7 overleaf.

Illustration 5 Impact of a 5% increase in prices

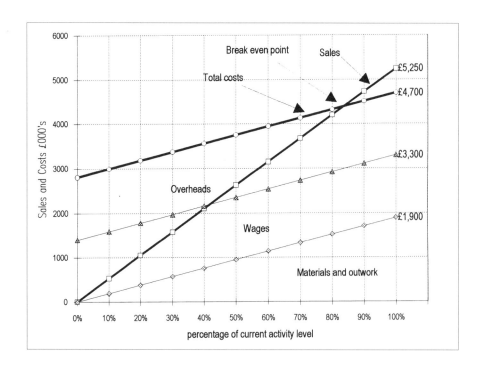

Illustration 6 Impact of a 5% reduction in either direct wages or overheads

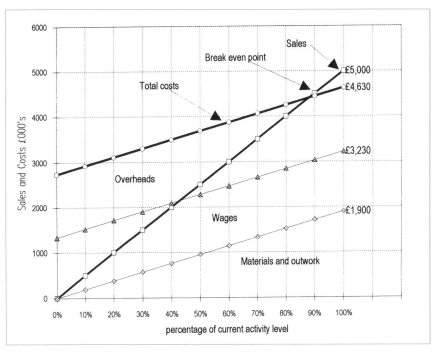

Illustration 7 Impact of 5% changes in sales, prices and wages

	Current year	5% increase in volume	5% increase in prices	5% cut in wages
Sales	5000	5250	5250	5000
Materials	1500	1575	1500	1500
Outwork	400	420	400	400
Value added	3100	3255	3350	3100
Wages	1400	1400	1400	1330
Contribution	1700	1855	1950	1770
Overheads	1400	1400	1400	1400
Net profit	300	455	550	370
Net profit/ Sales %	6.00%	8.67%	10.48%	7.40%

13

1.16 What these figures demonstrate is that relatively small increases in sales have a disproportionate effect on profits. For example a 5% increase in sales has resulted in increases in net profits of 52%, where the sales increase was due to higher volume, and of 83% where the sales increase was due to a price increase, whereas a 5% reduction in costs resulted in only a 23% increase in profits. This is quite significant for it draws attention to the need to be constantly looking to increase sales and hence value added. This means having a sales force that is properly targeted and motivated and also a pricing policy that is geared to generating sales that produce the highest value added to wages ratios.

1.18 The matrix in illustration 8 shows the impact of combinations of changes in prices and volume on profits where current sales are £5,000,000 and profits £300,000. Reading along the top line, a 5% increase in volume combined with a 5% reduction in prices would result in a fall in profits from £300,000 to £193,000. This is an important warning about the effects of a price reduction on profits if the resultant increase in volume sales is insufficient to offset it. A 5% increase in volume with no change in prices would result in an increase in profits to £455,000, while a 5% increase in both volume and prices would result in an increase in profits to £718,000 more than double current profits.

1.19 Reading along the bottom line, a 5% reduction in volume combined with a 5% reduction in price would result in a loss of £93,000 . A 5% reduction in volume with no change in price would result in a fall in profits to £145,000, whereas a fall in volume of 5% offset by a 5% increase in price would result in an increase in profits from £300,000 to £382,000. Thus provided that it is not offset by a substantial fall in volume a price increase could result in increased profits.

Illustration 8 The impact of changes in prices and volume on profits

Profits £000s

Volume change	Price Change										
	5%	4%	3%	2%	1%	0%	-1%	-2%	-3%	-4%	-5%
5%	718	665	613	560	508	455	403	350	298	245	193
4%	684	632	580	528	476	424	372	320	268	216	164
3%	651	599	548	496	445	393	342	290	239	187	136
2%	617	566	515	464	413	362	311	260	209	158	107
1%	584	533	483	432	382	331	281	230	180	129	79
0%	550	500	450	400	350	300	250	200	150	100	50
-1%	516	467	417	368	318	269	220	170	120	71	21
-2%	483	434	385	336	287	238	189	140	91	42	-7
-3%	449	401	352	304	255	207	159	110	61	13	-36
-4%	416	368	320	272	224	176	128	80	32	-16	-64
-5%	382	335	287	240	192	145	98	50	2	-45	-93

	£000s
Current sales	5000
Purchases	1900
Value added	3100
Wages	1400
Contribution	1700
Overheads	1400
Net profit	300

1.20 The figures in this matrix apply simply to the hypothetical firm with the sales and cost structure shown at the foot of the matrix. But a similar matrix could be drawn up for any other firm with any other sales and cost structure as a useful guide to the impact on their profits of changes in prices and volume.

Ways of increasing value added

1.21 There are a number of ways of increasing value added. A straight increase in volume sales will produce an increase in added value at a higher level of utilisation. Selling the same volume but at higher prices will also increase value added without requiring an increase in utilisation. Paying less for raw materials or using them more efficiently by cutting out waste also increases value added without requiring higher utilisation. Paying less in wages does not increase value added, although contribution will be increased.

1.22 Thinking in terms of value added helps in understanding the implications of prices changes. For example, if a product has a high materials content a small fall in price will produce a disproportionately large reduction in value added. If it has a relatively low materials content then a small increase in price will produce a disproportionately large increase in value added. In a company with relatively stable fixed costs the way to improve profitability is to increase value added. This can be done by increasing the volume of sales, by selectively increasing prices, and by altering the mix of work so as to increase the proportion of products with a low materials content and/or a high value added:wages content.

1.23 A company should be looking all the time to increase value added. To do this through a marketing approach requires a systematic analysis of sales by products and the markets into which they are being sold and the value added and contribution which each "product/market" is generating. This will enable "product/markets" to be listed in order of value added and contribution generated. A firm c an then start to redirect its marketing and selling effort to maximise/optimise sales into those "product/markets" which generate the highest value added ratios.

- Performance ratios based on value added

1.24 The information provided by the value added and contribution analysis of management accounts enables the calculation of some important ratios which can be used to monitor a company's performance. The ratios are:

- Value added/sales %
- Value added:wages
- Contribution/sales %
- Contribution/value added %

- Value added/sales

1.25 Value added/sales measures the proportion of sales being retained within the firm. This will vary depending on the type of business, whether customers supply any of the materials, the amount of outwork etc. There is no single industry "best" target figure at which a firm should be aiming, but it should be monitoring its own ratio and aiming to increase it.

- Value added : wages

1.26 Value added:wages measures how much value added is being generated per £ spent on wages. It is in part a measure of production efficiency, with the proviso that the value added part of the equation is influenced by factors not directly related to production e.g. sales volume and prices, raw material prices and outwork. Again there is no specific industry "best" target figure at which a firm should be aiming; but it should be aiming to improve on current performance. The more capital intensive the operation the higher the figure needs to be because the ratio of overheads, including depreciation, to direct wages will be that much higher than in a firm which is labour intensive.

- Contribution/sales

1.27 Contribution/sales measures the proportion of sales available to meet overheads and provide for profits and is a combination of the previous two ratios. Again there is no target figure at which a firm should be aiming, other than an improvement on the current performance.

- Contribution/value added

1.28 Contribution/value added is the inverse of the previous ratio and is calculated for convenience when it comes to plotting the ratios on a contribution contour grid and will be demonstrated later.

1.29 We say that there are no specific target figures at which firms should be aiming. But this is true only in the sense that there are no figures which can be universals quoted as targets, because each firm is different. But as we shall see later, when a firm comes to draw up its business plan and marketing strategy there will be a target figure for each performance ratio at which it must aim if it is to achieve the profit objective set in the business plan.

1.30 The performance ratios are easy to calculate from the value added analysis of the management accounts in paragraph 1.07 as follows:

Value added/sales	3100/5000 x 100 = 62.0%
Value added : wages	3100/1400 = 2.21
Contribution/sales	1700/5000 x 100 = 34.0%
Contribution/value added	1700/3100 x 100 = 54.8%

- Assessing performance

1.31 The productivity of companies is often evaluated by sales per head or other factors which can be distorted by extraneous elements. Experience indicates that such measures can give grossly misleading results, especially where inter-company and inter-country comparisons are made. Measures need to be self compensating for inflation and currency fluctuations. Measures based on value added compensate for different materials usage, and comparing value added with the cost of direct labour used rather than numbers of employees enables productivity comparisons to be made with a built in compensation for inflation.

1.32 Using value added:wages serves a dual purpose. It measures the effectiveness of the organisation in obtaining the appropriate mix of work and the effectiveness of the production department in producing that work. It therefore measures the financial effectiveness of the resources employed and can be used as a measure of wage productivity.

1.33 However, the use of a single measure can be misleading in the same way that a single co-ordinate for a map reference can be misleading. Just as one needs both longitude and latitude references to locate oneself on a map, so a company requires two performance ratios to determine its performance. As value added is so heavily influenced by materials usage then a monitor of materials performance can be very helpful. Certainly experience suggests that insufficient note is taken of material and sub-contracting trends. A second co-ordinate, that of value added to sales, fills this need.

1.34 But it is best if all three performance ratios are taken into account when assessing a firm's performance. As the following example demonstrates, it is not sufficient to base an assessment on a single ratio.

1.35 Let us assume that a printing firm employs 10 production workers at an hourly wage cost of £10 for a working week of 40 hours. Labour utilisation is estimated at 80%, i.e. a total of 320 chargeable hours per week. The firm produces two types of print job A and B with each job requiring different inputs of materials and outwork and taking different times on the press.

Illustration 9a The importance of using all three ratios

	Type A £	Type B £
Sales value	1000	1000
less materials and outwork	300	100
= Value added	700	900
Value added/sales	70%	90%
Time taken to do the job	14hrs	40hrs
Direct wage cost	140	400
Value added : wages	5.00	2.25

The Power of Added Value

1.36 Looking at only two ratios we find that type B work "wins" in terms of value added/sales and that type A work "wins" in terms of value added:wages. We therefore need to look also at contribution/sales which we can do by assuming that the firm can switch all of its production in one week to one or other of the two types of work as follows:

Illustration 9b The importance of using all three ratios

	Type A £	Type B £
Chargeable wages (320hrs @ £10)	3200	3200
Value added per £ of wages	5.00	2.25
Value added	16000	7200
Value added/sales %	70%	90%
Therefore sales value of work done	22857	8000

Deduct from value added actual wages paid of £4000

= Contribution	12000	3200
Contribution/sales	52.5%	40.0%

1.37 Thus type A work gives a higher contribution/sales performance ratio because of the superior value added:wages achieved on that type of work. Where labour is a limiting factor and the firm is operating at or near capacity it is important that it should take type A work in preference to type B work if it has a choice.

- Performance ratios as a guide to decision making and action

1.38 Performance ratios can be used to guide decision making in a number of areas, but it is important first to understand the various factors affecting each ratio. It

21

cannot be emphasised too strongly that each ratio has both a numerator and a denominator and that both affect the ratio. In illustration 10 we show the various factors influencing two of the ratios - value added/sales and value added:wages. The third ratio - contribution/sales is a function of the other two and therefore subject to all the factors influencing them.

1.39 Taking the value added/sales ratio first. This ratio is influenced on the sales side by the firm's sales strategies which determine what type of products the firm makes and the markets they are sold into, by the mix of products within total sales, and by the firm's pricing policies which determine how much each product shall be sold for and therefore indirectly how many will be sold, i.e. the volume of sales and the price. How much value added is generated out of those sales will be influenced by how much needs to be spent on materials, i.e. the firm's purchasing policies, how much material is wasted in the production process and hence quality control procedures, and by the firm's policy on outwork. A "poor" value added/sales ratio therefore should direct attention initially to all these influences.

1.40 The value added:wages ratio is influenced by all those factors which influence the value added/sales ratios plus a number of other factors which influence the wages part of the equation. These include the firm's wages policies - is it a high, low or average payer; the level of utilisation - how well is the wage bill being used up in saleable production; manning levels; and production control systems which ensure a steady flow of work through the production processes. A "poor" value added:wages ratio therefore should direct attention not only at the firm's production facilities and efficiencies but also at its ability to generate value added through sales.

Illustration 10 Factors influencing performance ratios

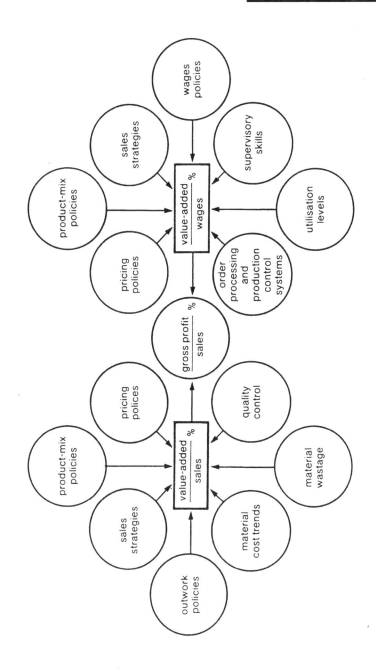

1.41 If we go back to the examples of the impact of 5% increases in volume, prices and wages we find the following performance ratios would be achieved:

Illustration 11 Impact on performance ratios of 5% changes in sales volume, prices and wages

Performance ratios	Current year	5% increase in volume	5% increase in prices	5% cut in wages
Value added/sales %	62.0%	62.0%	63.8%	62.0%
Value added: wages	2.21	2.33	2.39	2.33
Contribution/sales %	34.0%	35.3%	37.1%	35.4%
Contribution/value added	54.8%	57.0%	58.2%	57.1%

1.42 Clearly the best improvement comes from a price increase. But how to achieve a price increase, that is the problem. Across the board price increases are introduced in the printing industry, but these are usually in response to a similar increase in paper prices or following on the annual round of wage negotiations so there might be little or no change in the respective ratios as a result. Price increases that improve the performance ratios have to be more subtle than that.

1.43 We have to think of "price" in this context as being the sales value per unit of utilisation, the unit in this case being the average hourly wage rate. If we go back to paras. 1.30 - 1.33 we recall that a printer had the option of producing two types of product, type A giving a substantially higher value added:wages performance ratio than type B. It was clearly beneficial for the printer to maximise his output of type A products at the expense of type B products. All that is necessary is for the printer to be able to identify which of his products (and markets) are type A and which type B.

1.44 A good management information system, therefore, should show for each job done and for each quotation made the value added and contribution they generate and should record that information on the cost sheet. The system should also store this information in a databank that will enable it to be analysed by type of product and by market, showing the performance ratios generated by each job, by products, by markets and by product/market cells. How to collect this information is the subject of the next two chapters.

CHAPTER 2

MARKET SEGMENTATION

- Getting away from process orientation

2.01 Printing firms tend to be production/process orientated rather than product/market orientated. They tend to regard themselves as litho printers, gravure houses, four colour printers etc. Less often do they think in terms of the products they produce, though clearly they produce very specific products such as books, periodicals, business forms, cheque books, cartons etc. Even less often do they think of themselves in terms of the markets they supply though clearly these various markets are very different, have very specific needs and are the printer's source of revenue.

2.02 The versatility of printing machines, the ability to print almost anything for anybody fosters this production/process orientation. As a result firms tend to be inward looking, concerned more with the production process than with the products they are making and the markets they are supplying.

2.03 Attitudes become constrained. A view is held that only through production can a firm survive. Information is restricted and inward looking, concerned only with costs, machine running times, etc. Prices are based on costs and not on what the market will bear. Cost cutting exercises are seen as the only way of improving profits.

2.04 Because printing has had for 500 years or so a monopoly in the storage and retrieval of information, managerial emphasis has been placed on effective production. The demand has always been there. All a well

27

managed firm has had to do has been to organise its production efficiently to service that demand. But times have now changed, printing firms are no longer simply competing amongst themselves but are competing with other industries. Therefore they have to become much more market orientated and much more proactive in their approach to markets and potential customers.

2.05 The printing industry has come to be regarded as a service industry. But it is a manufacturing industry, with the demand for its products derived from the activities of its customers. It can rarely make for stock to iron out fluctuations in demand. These have to be accommodated by overtime working on the one hand and excess capacity on the other.

2.06 In order to become less reactive and to improve levels of profitability, printers have to start directing their activities towards those sections of the market place which they are best able to serve and which give them the best returns. They have to start analysing their markets and how they are developing. They have to identify those products which best meet the needs of those markets which produce the best returns. They have to identify particular customers and their needs and aim to satisfy them.

2.07 A firm has to be looking for opportunities in those markets which will give it the best return on the resources at its disposal . This means examining the products it can manufacture, deciding what it is best at, finding where the opportunities are in the market place for those products, identifying existing and potential new customers, and assessing how their needs might change and develop.

- Market segmentation

2.08 Market segmentation is the first step in the systematic approach to structuring and then analysing the information in a company 's information systems. It involves building up a bank of information about markets and products. The information can then be used to assess various options and determine courses of action.

2.09 Taking this step usually requires a shift in attitudes away from the production orientation of most firms towards the marketing orientation of the more successful firms. The shift has to be right across the organisation and not just confined to the sales director and/or managing director. One of the most important characteristics of the successful firms was the external focus of the whole organisation and not just those directly in contact with the customers.

- The market place for print

2.10 The printing industry is a manufacturing industry, in 1993 worth more than £8bn. Printers manufacture products. They supply 10,000 copies of a brochure not 10,000 copies of "service". Yet many printers regard themselves as providing a service and this influences their approach to the market-place. They tend to have a passive response to the market-place, waiting for the business to come in to the organisation and offering and accepting to do almost anything for anybody. They have tended not to specialise except perhaps in terms of the production processes.

2.11 The "anything for anybody" approach leaves the printer with very little control over the customers with whom he deals - he is al most wholly reactive to them, he has little or no control over the products he manufactures and little or no control over production . The commercial implications are fairly significant. Specialisation and an understanding of the market in which the firm is operating has become increasingly important. The ability to identify key market areas and key buyer groups enables firms to react more quic kly to shifts in the market and changes in the levels of activity in different industries and geographical areas. It enables them to keep a finger on the pulse.

2.12 The main disadvantage of the "anything for anybody" approach is that a firm cannot develop any specialist knowledge of the markets it serves. It cannot start to differentiate its products and services from those of its competitors. It cannot start to add value to its products by knowing more about its customers' requirements. The only factor which differentiates it from competitors is price.

2.13 Firms which specialise can start to do all these things. They can start to differentiate themselves from their competitors in more ways than just price. How do they set about doing it? How do they start to identify and segment the markets they are in and the products they produce in such a way as to use the information to focus their activities and generate more business?

- Defining a market

2.14 By and large printers are in an industrial market. They are supplying goods and services to other manufacturers or providers of services whose needs are motivated by profit and by the demand for their own products. Demand for printers' products is what is called "derived demand". It is derived from the business activities of its customers. In this respect it is a barometer of general business activity. Relatively few printers are selling direct to the public and therefore able to affect the level of demand directly. Printers' products and sales are very largely locked into the activities of other industries, firms and institutions.

2.15 This £8bn market can be represented as a cube with along one axis the various products, along the second axis the various customer industries and end users and along the third axis their geographical location. The size of the cube is determined largely by the level of economic activity.

Illustration 12 The market for print

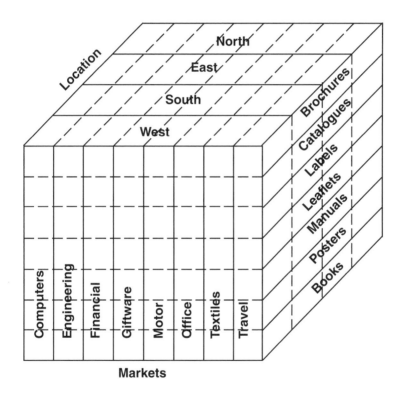

Markets

2.16 No one printer is large enough to influence the size of the cube. No one printer is so large that he can carve out a significant market share. But it is possible for an individual firm to carve out a niche for itself in a particular segment of the market. To do this it has to identify specific areas in the market-place - specific products across a range of customers, or a range of products into a specific group of customers or specific customers in a specific location. The firm can develop expertise in that market which enables it to tailor products to meet specific needs and hence to get out of the "price trap" which lies waiting for firms which find nothing to distinguish themselves from their competitors other than price.

2.17 There are dangers of course that particular markets will disappear or be drastically reduced. For example, the market for flat sheet multi part sets declined 50% in five years. But having an intimate knowledge of the market and how it is changing should help managers foresee such changes, caused in that case by product substitution. Both the returns and the risks might be high. It is necessary to have a sensitive finger on the pulse of the market. Having a thorough knowledge of the product and the purpose for which it is bought greatly helps in this respect.

2.18 The best way to start identifying the markets a firm is in is to run through the customer list placing each customer into a market category e.g. publishing, motor manufacturing, food processing etc. The Standard Industrial Trades Classification published by the HMSO can be used for this purpose as all firms are allocated an SITC code and can thus be identified by the industry they are in. It may of course be necessary to adapt the final categories to suit the individual firm's customer base.

- Defining a product

2.19 The printer is primarily selling a product. What is the customer buying? First of all he is buying a "physical product". He is buying a certain quantity of print on paper, products which have physical attributes including size of sheet, number of pages, amount of text, amount of colour, quality etc. These might be books, magazines, advertising leaflets, labels, cartons etc. Printers have to think in these terms and not as some still do in terms of being for example litho printers or four colour printers etc. For example one printer, 90% of whose output was labels, saw himself as a four colour printer.

2.20 While it is relatively easy to define what a customer is buying - the "physical or tangible product", it is less easy to define why a customer is buying a particular product - the "beneficial product". But it is necessary to do so in order to understand the reasons for purchases and the factors that will influence those purchases. If the "benefit" to the customer disappears so will the need to purchase the product. Substitution might also take place because another product better serves the need. There is little point in being the best producer of mousetraps if no-one has a rodent problem.

2.21 A key step in defining a product therefore is thinking through why the customer is buying it. What is the "benefit" to the customer? Company accounts are a legal requirement on companies. To satisfy that legal requirement companies need only present their accounts in a certain way and have them simply typed out and printed up. But many companies go in for a glossy version which goes far beyond the legal requirement. They are in fact using the accounts for promotional purposes. A book is a means of communication either for information or entertainment purposes. There might be alternative ways of communicating the same information or alternative form s of entertainment. Bingo tickets are bought to satisfy an urge to gamble. Packaging was bought to protect products but has become increasingly important as a means of promoting those products.

2.22 The use to which the customer puts the printed product - the "beneficial product" has an important influence on what he is prepared to pay for it and the standards of printing in respect of quality etc which he demands of the printer.

2.23 The third step in defining a product is to identify the reasons why the customer is buying it from your firm and not from your competitors. What characteristics do you have as a supplier which cause customers to buy from your firm rather than competitors and thereby create your firm's share of the market? This is the "extended product" which might differ from customer to customer and market to market.

2.24 Many printers would simply answer "service" without actually defining what they mean by "service", beyond perhaps "telling the customer that we are going to be late"! But customers expect all their suppliers to deliver on time. What the printer needs to be doing is identifying those aspects of "service" which differentiate him from his competitors. This means thinking in terms of what individual customers need. It means thinking about the customer's business and what he requires from his printer to make him more competitive. Does he need an overnight service such as that provided by city printers, is security all important, does he need to make last minute changes to prices quoted in brochures, does he need fast reprint service, does he require stockholding for call off? These and more are the questions printers need to ask about their customers and about the service they are providing.

2.25 While the total market for printed products - the "beneficial product" - is by and large determined by factors outside the individual printer's control, the share that he has of that market is determined by how well he produces the product - the "physical or tangible product", what service he offers - the ..."extended product", and what he charges for it.

- Looking at the end usage, "what business are we in?"

2.26 The printer can now start to ask the question "what business are we in?" The quick answer is "communications" or "the storage and retrieval of information". But the printer is really in the business of his customer and the demands of that business will vary. The city printer is in the financial business. The business ethos is that of the merchant banks and other financial institutions. If he is to be successful he must understand and work to that ethos. That applies equally to publishing, to the magazine world, to the advertising world, to the pharmaceutical industry and to any other to which the printer sells.

2.27 Some printers do this systematically while others do it informally. But very often the markets which printers find themselves in are the result of historical accidents and response to customers rather than the specific focusing of their own marketing effort. But the advantages of targeting markets are obvious. Firms start to develop a level of expertise in the market, they understand the language, they start to get referrals from other firms in the same industry as purchasing managers tend to move around within the same industry and also pass on recommendations.

2.28 Most printers tend to organise their sales forces on a geographical or product basis, few on an industry or type of customer basis. The advantages of targeting salespersons on particular industries or types of customer are that they come to understand the particular needs of an industry, the customers' reasons for buying, the "benefits", the service requirements, the developments taking place which are likely to affect demand, the possibilities of substitution. The method of analysing sales set out in subsequent chapters is designed to help firms target their salesforces.

- Constructing a product/market matrix

2.29 Having started to think in terms of products and markets the next step is to construct a product/market matrix. The purpose in analysing the market place this way is to answer the question "what and whose business are we in?" It provides the basis for identifying market opportunities and threats and for assessing strengths and weaknesses and the ability to respond to market opportunities. It also provides the basic structure for coding up each job the company has done and will do in the future and then analysing each job's performance in terms of the value added they generate.

2.30 The product/market matrix is set up with products listed along the vertical axis and markets/customers listed along the horizontal axis. A ten by ten matrix giving a hundred cells should be sufficient but will vary depending on a firm's range of products and customers, and many firms may find that they need a much larger matrix. Careful thought needs to be given to the definition of products to ensure that they are both market orientated and relevant to the firm's production processes. For example the product might be cartons, but some might be glued and others produced as flats with significantly different costs involved so they might need to be distinguished separately. The product might also require more than one pass on a machine which could significantly affect the cost of production. This also should be taken into account and perhaps the products also distinguished separately.

2.31 The basic aim should be to identify discrete products that the firm produces. The main criterion should be the reason for the purchase. If the product is to serve a different need then it should be categorised separately whether or not it can be produced on the same machine. Coloured forms and coloured leaflets are a case in point for their uses are entirely different.

2.32 The identification of markets should be approached using the customer list, with each customer being allocated to a specific market as defined for example by the Standard Industrial Trades Classification. Large customers accounting for a significant proportion of sales can be regarded as a separate "market".

2.33 An example of a product/market matrix is shown at illustration 13 overleaf.

2.34 This product/market matrix is fundamental to the development of a marketing strategy and a key feature of the management information system. It encourages management to start thinking in terms of market segmentation, it enables sales to be analysed by product and market and it provides the framework for the value added analysis of individual jobs that will be the subject of the next chapter.

2.35 Any analysis of immediate past performance will start from this matrix. Each job completed will need to be given both a product and a market code so that it can be entered into the management information system and allocated to a particular product/market cell within the matrix. This will enable a product/market analysis of sales to be made on the one hand, and a detailed value added analysis by product, market and product/market cell on the other. Furthermore each new job done in the future will also be allocated appropriate codes so that information on it can be entered in the appropriate cell and information for each cell and for each product and market can then be aggregated using the management information system.

- Product/market analysis of sales

2.36 The past year's sales can now be analysed by product, by market and by product/market cell with each

Illustration 13 A product/market matrix

Products/ Markets	Brochures £	Catalogues £	Greetings £	Labels £	Leaflets £	Manuals £	Posters £	Total £
Computers	250000			150000		85750		235750
Engineering					145000	115500		510500
Financial	303750		175000					478750
Giftware			120000	90000			85000	295000
Motor	400000				165000	30000	85000	680000
Office			125000	70000				195000
Pharmaceuticals				375000	310000			685000
Public bodies				70000	220000			290000
Textiles		700000		190000				890000
Travel	275000	180000		75000			210000	740000
Total	1228750	880000	420000	1020000	840000	231250	380000	5000000

job done during the year allocated the appropriate product and market codes and the sales values recorded. This analysis will establish which products are being sold into which markets and the total values of those sales. The relative importance of each product and market within the firm's overall activities will become clear. The 80/20 rule will probably apply with 80% of sales being accounted for by the four or five markets.

2.37 It is unlikely that all the cells will have something in them. The fewer the number of cells with something in them the more concentrated the firm's marketing effort is likely to have been. The higher the number of cells with sales recorded in them the more diffuse and unfocussed the firm's selling efforts are likely to have been.

2.38 A firm can now identify its main products, its main markets and its main customers. It can also start to analyse in qualitative terms what the main influences on those markets are, what external factors are influencing the markets, which markets offer opportunities for increased sales, which markets are stagnating or under threat, what the competition is doing, and what the firm itself has to do to take advantage of opportunities. Is this a matter of price, is it a matter of quality or of service?

- Identifying opportunities

2.39 It now becomes possible to start looking at individual markets in terms of their potential for growth and the share which the firm has of a particular market. The markets can be divided up into those that are growing, those that are stagnating and those that are declining on the one hand, and those in which the firm has a small market share and those in which it has a large market share on the other. A firm can start to look through "the window" at what is happening outside the business, instead of looking simply at what is happening inside of the business. In gearing the resources of the business to meet the needs of the market it is necessary to have a clear understanding of who buys what and why. The reasons customers have for buying certain products will determine the likely future shape of demand, whether the demand will increase or decline.

2.40 The product/market analysis identifies not only current activities but also potential market opportunities that are not being met. By extending the matrix it is possible to identify potential areas for product/market diversification.

2.41 The value to the company of some product/market combinations might be immediately obvious. But before decisions are taken comprehensive marketing information should be gathered for each product/market cell along with forecasts of likely future demand. The information for this market audit should include facts about the seller, the buyer, market share, the competition, constraints, growth potential etc.

- Information about customers

2.42 In evaluating the market place, information about customers is important. What are the characteristics of the firm's customers? What are the trends in the market? What is happening to its customers' business? What is happening to the business the customer places with us? Is there a difference between internal trends and external trends?

- Information about the competition

2.43 Success in a particular product/market area will be influenced by the activities of competitors. The competition is not only other printers but other products and services that fill the same need. Competition can be divided into three types:

- ENTERPRISE COMPETITION - that is other organisations that offer the same goods and services to the same markets.

- PRODUCT FORM COMPETITION - things of a similar form but produced by different methods and enterprises. Copying machines are an example of this.

- BENEFICIAL COMPETITION - often the most difficult to identify and likely to do the most damage. Computers are beneficial competition as are tape recorders. The beneficial competition relates to the beneficial product.

- Information on constraints

2.44 This information should cover factors that might stop or discourage a potential buyer from buying. It should also cover social and economic factors over which the buyer and seller have no control e.g. economic legislation etc. but which might affect purchasing decisions.

- Information on channels of distribution and the end user

2.45 Suppliers and manufacturers are often more than one step removed from the final user - who ultimately determines demand. Information about the channels of distribution, the costs and the benefits, is an important ingredient in ensuring customer satisfaction. There is also a need to know about the end user as well as the immediate customer.

- Specialisation

2.46 The marketing approach of identifying current product/ market combinations and forecasting opportunities enables management to identify those areas where commercial activity should be concentrated. The aim of specialisation is to distinguish the company from the competition and to remove it from the price war.

2.47 The decision as to where to sell a product is of equal importance to the decision about which products to sell. It depends on whether a company is aiming to optimise its existing operations or introduce a totally new product line with new customers.

2.48 The success or failure of a firm ultimately depends upon obtaining and keeping profitable, satisfied customers. The firm, therefore, stands a greater chance of being successful if it can find the right sort of potential customers rather than waiting for the customer to find him. The nature and location of the customer is defined by the nature of the product the company makes or is considering making. The feasibility of supplying the customer is determined by a number of external environmental factors that bear directly or indirectly on the market. Experience suggests that because of inadequate information firms adapt slowly to a changing environment, sometimes with serious results. Firms therefore need to identify potential customers, their location and number, the areas of operation, the channels of distribution and continually monitor the market if they are to improve their performance.

- Market knowledge

2.49 What does a firm need to know about its markets? A typical printer's customers might include government and other public bodies, advertising agents, industrial firms and direct consumers. The market conditions in these different market areas will vary widely. It is important therefore for a printer to know the number, location and spending power of potential customers.

2.50 The attractiveness or otherwise of a particular market to a firm will depend upon the existing market conditions. For example, in the industrial market there may be intense local competition aiming at a few firms, but within striking distance there may be a large market that is not being satisfactorily served by printers in that locality. In specialist product areas the market may be national and even international. Whilst the activities of competitors will be important, the choice of distribution channels will also be important in ensuring satisfactory market conditions and overcoming competition. In monitoring market conditions, therefore, a fir m has to know about direct and indirect competitors activities, channels of distribution and agencies, sources of supply of materials - vitally important if customer satisfaction is to be assured - and the effects on the customer of the location of the firm.

2.51 More general factors can also have a significant effect on a firm's choice of markets and customers. They include the state of the economy, technological changes, the political climate and local culture. The economic environment has a significant effect. It i s also well known that customers tend to prefer to purchase locally, a factor particularly important in overseas markets.

2.52 However the decision about customers is made, the wider the view that is taken of the market the better informed will be that decision. To do the job, a sensitive information system is needed which co-ordinates information that exists within the firm and the mass of data available outside the firm. Key figures in this information system are the sales personnel who should be bringing in information about developments in particular markets. Sales personnel who are organised on a market rather than geographical or product basis are likely to bring in the better information about market developments.

2.53 The next step is to identify the underlying need behind the purchase of the product in each separate market. For example, take sales of multipart sets. The need behind a transport firm' purchases of multipart sets would be to satisfy international requirement s for the transport of goods across international frontiers. The level of demand is affected by the level of trade and by the fact that it is a legal requirement. The total level of demand is not affected by price.

2.54 The need behind banks' purchases of multipart sets would be to facilitate the transmission of money. This too is determined by the level of economic activity, but this need is increasingly being met by electronic means. There is therefore a threat to multipart sets in that particular market. Price might be more of an influence on overall demand.

2.55 An analysis such as this has to be carried out step by step for each product in each market. It is hard work and a time consuming exercise but necessary if the firm is to start to understanding the various factors influencing demand in different markets and hence to start pricing for those markets. It becomes necessary to build up an adequate information system to provide this information .

2.56 When all the information has been assembled it will be possible to group current sales - products into markets - under four headings:

- a high market share in a high growth market (a 'star')

- a low market share in a high growth market (a 'question mark')

- a high market share in a low growth market (a cash 'cow')

- a low market share in a low growth market (a 'dog')

2.57 An assessment can start to be made of where the opportunities and threats lie: which markets are expanding and which declining; in which markets will it be possible to increase market share either by selling more of the same products to existing customers or to new customers; in which markets are sales under threat from competitors or new products; are there opportunities to start selling new products into existing markets or more riskily new products into new markets?

2.58 Each of these options has a different risk factor, different implications for pricing and different implications for investment and hence cash flow. The option with the lowest risk factor is selling existing products to existing customers. The next is selling existing products to new customers, followed by selling new products into existing markets. The option with the highest risk factor is selling new products to new markets.

2.59 The timescales over which these various options can be taken up also differ. In the short term the only available and safest option is to consolidate by selling more of the same products to existing customers and to new customers in the same markets. In the medium term the option of selling the same products into new markets becomes more feasible. In the longer term it is wise to be looking at the option of developing new products which might be sold into existing or new markets.

- The marketing approach to profit generation

2.60 A company aiming to increase its net profits can try to regulate and if possible reduce its various expenses. Alternatively it can try to improve its contribution. It has a number of options:

• to increase sales volume;

• to manage the sales mix so as to increase the proportion of value added to sales;

• to develop more sensitive pricing policies;

• to manage production so as to improve productivity and/ or reduce the incremental costs of work done;

2.61 To do this, management needs a good information system which provides data on the value added and contribution obtained from each individual job done. Without this knowledge management cannot make informed and rational choices. With this knowledge management can start to identify those niches in the market which it can supply most profitably. A production/process orientated company has internal cost centres. A company which intends to become market orientated needs to think in terms of external price centres which in effect are the different product/market cells identified by the product/ market matrix. Moreover management needs to have just as much if not more information about these external price centres than it has about its internal cost centres if it is to properly manage its marketing and sales effort.

2.62 Using the information from its external price centres management can begin to identify those products and markets that the company can supply most profitably and which offer the best opportunities for growth. They can also begin to establish what scope the company has for adjusting its prices in order to capture work in those markets.

2.63 The advantage of aiming for segments of the market in which the company is proficient is that the company comes to benefit from being on the "experience curve" rather than the "learning curve". A firm on the "experience curve" has the dual advantages of an under lying reduction in cost resulting from repetition and of knowing the needs of the market better. Whereas a firm accepting jobs from anywhere and not specialising remains on the "learning curve" unable to reduce costs and also never gaining detailed knowledge of particular markets.

2.64 In the short term, if profits are to be improved a firm has to be looking not simply to increasing sales of existing products into existing markets, but to increasing sales of those products into those markets which bring in the best returns. A simple drive to increase sales will not be as effective as this more targeted approach. How to identify which products and markets to target is the subject of chapter 4. It will require a further input from the management information system. Briefly it is a matter of establishing for each job done in each of the product/market cells, the worth of that work in terms of value added, contribution and performance ratios based on value added.

- Summary

2.65 The main steps in the market segmentation exercise are:

- Identify the different products which the firm produces;

- Identify the different markets into which the firm sells these products;

- Identify the individual customers and allocate them to the different markets, with very large customers being allocated their own "market";

- Construct a product/market matrix with products listed along the vertical axis and markets along the horizontal axis;

- Allocate sales to appropriate product/market cells and aggregate sales in each cell and in each horizontal line and vertical column;

- Identify major markets and products;

- Assemble information about the state of each market, growth potential and economic and other factors affecting that potential;

- Assemble information about your own firm's share of each market and the state of competition and assess potential for growth;

- Identify major customers in each market, establish their reasons for buying the product and why they buy from your firm;

- Identify potential growth areas and areas of stagnation and decline;

- Identify options for increasing sales.

CHAPTER 3

VALUE ADDED AND CONTRIBUTION ANALYSIS OF JOB SHEETS

- The use of value added and contribution analysis

3.01 The overall performance of the company as expressed in its annual management accounts is the sum of its performance on each of the jobs that it has done during the year. The total sales for the year are the sum of all the prices obtained for the individual jobs done, purchases for the year are the sum of the prices paid for the materials and outwork that have gone into those jobs. Likewise the three performance ratios which described the company's performance over the year are the sum of the performance ratios achieved on all the jobs done during the year.

3.02 Thus it is clear that in order to improve overall performance, a manager has to know the performance on each job, type of work and market. He can then start aiming to do more jobs with performance ratios above the average and fewer of those with ratios below the average so as to raise the overall average.

3.03 Some firms already use management information systems which will provide this information in a form that can be analysed and acted upon. Others may need to buy such a system or adapt and develop their own using one of the numerous database packages now on the market. Most of the data required should be found on the firm's individual job sheets and therefore already be available within the firm's existing information system.

49

3.04 Depending on the availability of information, the number of jobs done over a period and the availability of resources to enter the data, a firm can choose to analyse up to a year's worth of jobs already done, or it can set up the system to start collecting data in the appropriate form on all new jobs. Analysis can begin when a large enough sample is available - probably three months' worth of jobs.

3.05 In this chapter we explain what information needs to be pulled from the cost sheets and then how to analyse it. The stages in the process are as follows:

• Construction of a product /market matrix and coding of jobs;

• Calculation of an hourly wage only rate;

• Analysis of job sheets;

• Aggregation of job sheets by product, market and product/market cell and calculation of average performance ratios;

• Aggregation of all job sheets and calculation of overall average performance ratios for jobs done;

• Plotting of performance ratios for products, markets and product/market cells on contribution contour grid.

- Construction of product/market matrix and coding of jobs

3.06 In Chapter 2 we explained how to construct a product/ market matrix. This is central to value added and contribution analysis of job sheets because it enables each job to be coded by type of product and type of market. So each job should be given a product and market code in addition to the job number and customer reference it would normally have. These codes will identify each job by the type of product and the type of market as defined in the market segmentation exercise and make it possible for the database to produce aggregates for products, markets and product/market cells.

- Calculation of hourly wage only rate

3.07 For the value added and contribution analysis of job sheets to correspond exactly to the analysis of the management accounts we need to have a figure for the direct hourly wage only costs attributable to each job. Such a figure is not normally available from the industry's absorbed costing system which produces only a machine rate which includes overheads, or an hourly wage rate which takes no account of holidays. It will therefore be necessary to calculate an hourly wage only figure.

3.08 The first step is to draw up a list of all direct production employees (including assistants and trainees) in each production department together with information on their basic weekly wage, the National Insurance contribution paid on their behalf by the company and any pension contribution also paid by the company. The objective is to calculate an hourly wage only cost rate for each production department or "cost centre". The number of such "cost centres" should be kept to a minimum. For example, where there is flexible working within a department the department should be treated as a separate cost centre. Only where a particular machine is operated only by certain employees whose rates are very different from those of other employees in the department should a machine be regarded as a separate "cost centre". This data can be set up on a spreadsheet to facilitate the initial calculation and to enable any changes to be made as required as personnel and/or basic rates etc change.

3.09 The next step is to calculate the annual wage cost of each employee by adding together the weekly basic wage, NI contribution and pension fund contribution and multiplying by 52. If, for example, holiday pay or other bonus is automatically paid then this should be added to that sum. Overtime payments should not be included in this calculation unless the overtime working is in effect institutionalised and worked week in week out. The figures should then be summed to give the total annual wage cost for the department. An example is shown in illustration 15 for a press department with three machines run by three minders and two assistants.

3.10 Next, calculate the annual hours spent in the factory at normal rates by the direct production workers only, not the assistants. Overtime should not be included. For example, the normal working week may be 37.5 hours with 5 weeks annual leave and 1.6 weeks public holidays leaving 45.4 working weeks. The number of attendance hours therefore is 3 chargeable employees x 45.4 working weeks x 37.5 hours = 5107.5 hours.

3.11 The hourly wage only rate for the press department is therefore the total annual wage cost, £69,368, divided by 5107.5 hours which equals £13.58 per hour.

3.12 The "hourly wage only rate" should be calculated in the same way for each production department/cost centre and incorporated into the management information system. The wage cost of a job can then be calculated for each department it goes through and the costs aggregated to give a total wage cost for the job.

Illustration 14 Calculation of annual wage cost and hourly wage only rate

Press department

Employees	Basic weekly wage	Nat Ins & Serps	Pension weekly	Total year wage cost	Weeks/ yearly	Total wage cost
	£	£	£	£		£
A Minder	260.00	26.00	13.00	299.00	52	15548.00
B Minder	250.00	25.00	12.50	287.50	52	14950.00
C Minder	305.00	30.50	15.25	350.75	52	18239.00
A Assistant	165.00	16.50	8.25	189.75	52	9867.00
B Assistant	180.00	18.00	9.00	207.00	52	10764.00
				1334.00		69368.00

Employees	No. of chargeable employees	Hours/ week	Working weeks/ year	Working hours/ year	Hourly wage only rate
A Minder	1	37.5	45.4	1702.5	
B Minder	1	37.5	45.4	1702.5	
C Minder	1	37.5	45.4	1702.5	
	3	112.5	136.2	5107.5	£13.58

- Calculation of value added, contribution and performance ratios from job sheets

3.13 It will be recalled that in Chapter 1 we explained how to calculate value added and contribution from the management accounts. We took sales deducted purchases of raw materials and outwork to get value added and then deducted direct wages to arrive at contribution. We do the same calculation using the information on the job sheet. Illustration 15 provides an example of a job sheet designed as a database for calculating value added, contribution and the four performance ratios.

3.14 The actual job sheet used by an individual firm would of course be tailored to meet its specific needs. The basic need is to have enough relevant information on which to base marketing and operating decisions. The company in this example wants to be in a position to make decisions about operating through agents and also whether it should establish its own transport department.

3.15 Furthermore, as one of the purposes in collecting this information is to be able later to calculate "market prices", the selling price shown is what the customer pays for the job not what the printer receives after the agent has deducted his commission. So the commission paid to the agent is treated as an outwork cost. It should likewise be treated as an outwork cost in the analysis of the management accounts.

3.16 Under "wage costs" three departments are shown. The actual number and nomenclature of departments will of course depend on the particular circumstances of the firm. The "hourly wage only rate", which has been previously calculated (and is not to be confused with the "machine rate" found in the absorbed costing approach), is entered as a constant into the appropriate column for each department and multiplied by the number of hours the job takes in that department. The wage costs in each department are then aggregated and deducted from value added to arrive at contribution.

3.17 The performance ratios can then be calculated for each job showing how well it performed in terms of value added/sales, value added:wages and contribution/sales.

- Analysis of job sheets by product, market and product/market cell

3.18 Management information systems are now available with the programme written to handle the analysis of job sheets in this way and to aggregate the information as required for the purposes of analysing the performance of individual products, markets and product/market cells.

Illustration 15 Job Sheet database for measuring the worth of work

JOB NUMBER	CUSTOMER CODE
PRODUCT CODE	MARKET CODE £

Selling price (S)	5000
Purchases	
Materials	1500
Outwork	
Agents' commission	250
Pre-press	
Press	
Finishing	225
Transport	25
Total outwork	500
Total Purchases (P)	2000

Illustration 15 Job Sheet database for measuring the worth of work (continued)

Value added (VA)			3000

Wage costs

	Hours	Hrly. wage only rate	Wage cost
Pre-press	30	15.00	450.00
Press	20	13.58	271.60
Finishing			0

Total wage costs (W)	721.60
Contribution (C) = VA-W	2278.40

Performance ratios

Value added/sales (VA/Sx100)	60.0%
Value added:wages (VA/W)	4.16
Contribution/sales (C/Sx100)	45.6%
Contribution/value added (C/VAx100)	75.9%

3.19 The first step in the analysis is to aggregate the figures over the specific period chosen for comparison with the management accounts for the corresponding period, in this example the whole year. The aggregation can be done by products and by markets and the figures totalled to show the performance on all jobs done during the year. The jobs done in each product/market cell should also be aggregated and the performance ratios calculated. Examples are given at illustrations 16, 17 and 18.

3.20 Comparing the figures with those taken from the management accounts it can be seen that sales will be the same as also will be the cost of purchases of raw materials and outwork and hence value added. However, total wage costs arrived at by summing the individual jobs will be only about half the total wage costs shown in the management accounts. The reason for this is that no firm would be working flat out all the time with 100% utilisation. There are holidays which account for 12.7% of the wage bill plus downtime and waiting time of various sort and also overtime which is being paid for at time and a half or more. In other words the firm will not be recovering all its wage costs for the year on the jobs that are done during the year. The figure for contribution shown in the job sheet analysis will be higher than that in the management account by the difference between the two wage cost figures.

3.21 By dividing the wage cost figure derived from the cost sheet analysis by that derived from the management accounts one arrives at a "utilisation" rate for the period in question. In this example it works out at 50%. Typically in the printing industry utilisation is about 50-55%, with the better firms achieving 60-65%. Above that figure a firm would start to run into queuing problems unless the bulk of the work was of a periodic nature that could be scheduled well in advance.

3.22 The figure is a measure of the utilisation of the wages bill and is a useful indication of how efficiently the firm is operating and how well it is both managing the throughput and also selling into those markets which generate a high level of value added:wages and hence contribution. It is also a measure of the under-utilisation of the wages bill which reduces the final figure for contribution. In this context it draws attention for example to the advantages of bringing in house work which might previously have been bought as outwork. It also draws attention to the importance of managing overtime for part of the wages bill not recovered through jobs will represent overtime payments.

3.23 The figure calculated for utilisation becomes quite critical when we come to drawing up the business plan because an assumption will need to be made about the future level of utilisation which will in turn affect the overall value added:wages ratio that will need to be achieved in order to generate sufficient value added to meet the profit objective

3.24 Overall performance ratios can also be derived from the job sheet analysis by aggregating the sales, purchases and wages cost figures for all the jobs. The ratio for value added/sales will be the same as that derived from the management accounts. That for value added:wages and hence also that for contribution/sales derived from the job sheet analysis will be higher than those derived from the management accounts because the wage costs attributed to jobs will be lower than the total wages bill.

3.25 The figures should also be aggregated by product/market cell and the performance ratios calculated to show how each product is performing in each of the markets into which it is sold. A typical product/market cell for Brochures/Engineering is shown in illustration 18.

Illustration 16 Summary of job sheet analysis by product group

	Sales £	Purchases £	Value added £	Wages £	Contri-bution £	VA/S	VA:W	C/S	C/VA
Brochures	1228750	410000	818750	199000	619750	66.6%	4.11	50.4%	75.7%
Catalogues	880000	385000	495000	145000	350000	56.3%	3.41	39.8%	70.7%
Greetings	420000	158000	262000	54500	207500	62.4%	4.81	49.4%	79.2%
Labels	1020000	392000	628000	128500	499500	61.6%	4.89	49.0%	79.5%
Leaflets	840000	329000	511000	109000	402000	60.8%	4.69	47.9%	78.7%
Manuals	231250	60500	170750	31000	139750	73.8%	5.51	60.4%	81.8%
Posters	380000	165500	214500	33000	181500	56.4%	6.50	47.8%	84.6%
Total	5000000	1900000	3100000	700000	2400000	62.0%	4.43	48.0%	77.4%

Illustration 17 Summary of job sheet analysis by markets

	Sales £	Purchases £	Value added £	Wages £	Contri-bution £	VA/S	VA:W	C/S	C/VA
Computers	235750	63000	172750	29000	143750	73.3%	5.96	61.0%	83.2%
Engineering	510500	155000	355500	100500	255000	69.6%	3.54	50.0%	71.7%
Financial	478750	130000	348750	60000	288750	72.8%	5.81	60.3%	82.8%
Giftware	295000	143500	151500	24700	126800	51.4%	6.13	43.0%	83.7%
Motor	680000	203000	477000	113000	364000	70.1%	4.22	53.5%	76.3%
Office	195000	89000	106000	36800	69200	54.4%	2.88	35.5%	65.3%
Pharmaceuticals	685000	225000	460000	63000	397000	67.2%	7.30	58.0%	86.3%
Public bodies	290000	162500	127500	44000	83500	44.0%	2.90	28.8%	65.5%
Textiles	890000	391000	499000	162000	337000	56.1%	3.08	37.9%	67.5%
Travel	740000	338000	402000	67000	335000	54.3%	6.00	45.3%	83.3%
Total	5000000	1900000	3100000	700000	2400000	62.0%	4.43	48.0%	77.4%

Illustration 18 Product/market cell Brochures/Engineering

Order No.	Sales £	Purchases £	Value added £	Wages £	Contri-bution £	VA/S £	VA:W	C/S	C/VA
1001	30000	10000	20000	7500	12500	66.7%	2.67	41.7%	62.5%
1005	25000	8500	16500	5500	11000	66.0%	3.00	44.0%	66.7%
1010	20000	7500	12500	5500	7000	62.5%	2.27	35.0%	56.0%
1016	40000	12500	27500	5500	22000	68.8%	5.00	55.0%	80.0%
1023	80000	25000	55000	23000	32000	68.8%	2.39	40.0%	58.2%
1054	30000	9000	21000	4000	17000	70.0%	5.25	56.7%	81.0%
1067	25000	7500	17500	4000	13500	70.0%	4.38	54.0%	77.1%
Total	250000	80000	170000	55000	115000	68.0%	3.09	46.0%	67.6%

- The influence of the mix of work

3.26 This method of comparative analysis can be used to examine the different types of work obtained by a company, and to compare their performance one with another and against the overall company performance. Detailed analysis will show that different types of work have significantly different levels of performance depending upon the nature of the customer and the type of work produced.

3.27 This value added analysis will very likely show that there is no correlation between value added performance and cost sheet surplus and deficit calculated on an absorption costing basis. Furthermore the absorbed costing information might be very misleading as to the true value of the work to the company and may actually direct the manager away from the best route to profits.

3.28 The analysis also identifies the differences in the make up of the "contribution". Within any printing company jobs with a similar proportion of "contribution" can have a very different make up and hence value to the company. For example two jobs having a contribution/sales percentage of 40% could be quite different. The first could be made up totally of bought in work, bought for £600 and sold for £1000; whereas the second could be work using £100 of materials and direct wages of £500 and also selling for £1000.

3.29 This analysis which is the core of an effective pricing policy, would have been enormously time consuming if undertaken manually, but can now be done easily and quickly using a computer based management information system. Computers have changed many areas of company operation. They are particularly useful in pricing for bespoke work because the important features of a computer are used - memory capacity, speed of operation and consistency.

CHAPTER 4

CONTRIBUTION CONTOUR GRID ANALYSIS OF PRODUCTS AND MARKETS

4.01 We now have all the information we need to start analysing the firm's overall performance and the performance of individual products in individual markets. To carry out the analysis we need to plot the relevant information, i.e. the performance ratios, on a "contribution contour grid".

- Contribution contour grid

4.02 The contribution contour grid can be likened to an ordnance survey map with latitudes and longitudes locating your position on the map and the contour lines showing the height of your position above sea level. Corresponding to the latitude and longitude we have on the vertical axis value added/sales % and on the horizontal axis value added:wages which for ease of plotting is calculated as contribution/value added %. The contour lines are contribution/sales %. As explained earlier all three ratios are needed because each provides different information about performance. The same contribution/sales ratio could be achieved with various combinations of value added/sales and value added:wages ratios.

Illustration 19 Contribution contour grid

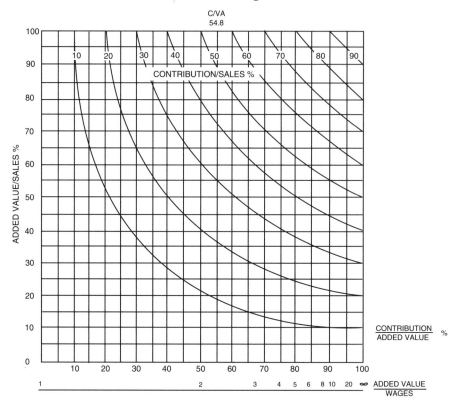

4.03 A firm's overall year end performance ratios can be plotted on this grid as shown in illustration 20. The value added/sales ratio is drawn with a horizontal line at 62.0% on the vertical axis, and the value added:wages ratio is drawn with a vertical line at 2.21 (contribution/value added = 54.8%) on the horizontal axis. Where the two lines cross is the contribution sales ratio of 34.0%, i.e. the firm's current overall performance position as pin-pointed by the three ratios.

Illustration 20 Contribution contour grid with overall year end performance ratios

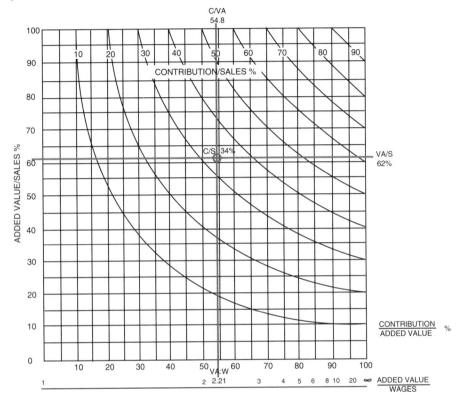

4.04 To improve on that position, to climb higher up the mountain of contribution contours, the firm has either to improve on its current value added/sales performance ratio or on its current value added:wages ratio or both. We have already identified in paras 1.34 and 1.35 and illustration 11 a number of the factors influencing the performance ratios and therefore have some ideas about what to do. The firm could do more jobs with a higher value added/sales ratio, reduce outwork or cut down on wastage. It could look generally at machine efficiencies and cut labour costs. But

65

as we have discovered earlier, the way to achieve significant improvements is to generate revenue through higher volume sales or higher prices. We therefore need to plot on the grid the performance ratios for individual products, markets and product/market cells which have been calculated from the analysis of job sheets to identify those that are generating the best ratios.

- Plotting overall job sheet performance

4.05 But first we plot the three ratios showing overall performance on all the jobs done in the period analysed. The value added/sales line should be the same as the line already drawn using the analysis of the management accounts, but the value added:wages line will be further to the right. The distance between the two value added:wages line will represent underutilisation of the wages bill.

- Plotting performance ratios for products, markets and product/ market cells

4.06 The next step is to plot on the grid the performance ratios for the individual products, markets and product/ market cells. Three separate grids will have to be used to avoid confusion. We show in illustration 22 the grid with the markets plotted. Each plot will fall into one or other of the four segments into which the grid has been divided by the overall performance lines.

4.07 Any product, market or product/market cell falling above the horizontal "overall performance" line is generating a value added/sales ratio that is better than average; while anything below the horizontal overall performance line is generating a value added/sale ratio that is below average. Anything to the right of the vertical "overall performance" line derived from the analysis of job sheets is generating a value added:wages ratio that is better than

Illustration 21 Contribution contour grid with the overall job sheet performance ratios added

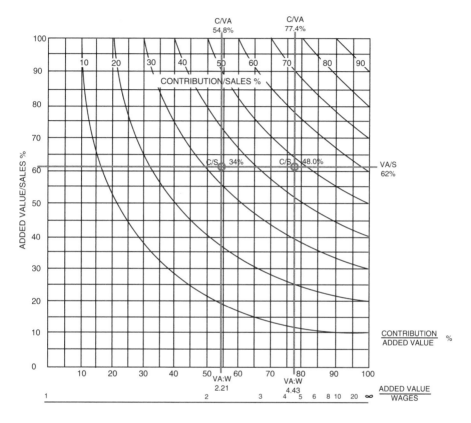

average. Anything to the left of that line but still to the right of the vertical year end "overall performance" line derived from the management accounts is worse than average compared with the jobs that have been done, but is still making a contribution. Anything to the left of the vertical year end "overall performance" line derived from the management accounts is actually detracting from overall performance.

Illustration 22 contribution contour grid with markets plotted

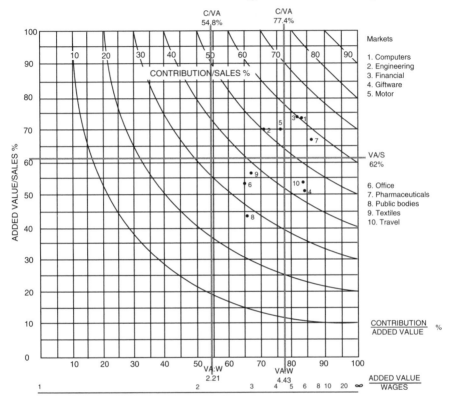

4.08 Clearly a company should be aiming to adjust its marketing mix so that the bulk of its products/markets fall into the top right hand segment of the grid. Products/ markets in this area are called "stars" and are better than average in terms both of materials utilising and wages productivity. Management should therefore be putting resources into developing sales of these products. Price can be used as a lever to increase sales because the value added:wages ratio is high and raw materials content is low.

4.09 Product/markets in the top left hand segment are generating above average value added/sales, but below average value added:wages. These are called "cash cows". Management needs to be looking to improving the efficiency of production of these products to bring their value added:wages performance closer to that of the "stars".

4.10 Product/markets in the bottom right hand segment are generating above average value added:wages but below average value added/sales. These are referred to as "question marks". Management needs to be looking to improve materials purchasing and usage or to bringing outwork in house. It should not be using price as a lever to increase sales because with a low value added/sales ratio a price reduction will cut added value substantially.

4.11 Product/markets in the bottom left hand segment are performing below average on both value added/sales and value added:wages and are referred to as "dogs". Management should be looking at these product/markets highly critically with a view to replacing them with better performers if their performance ratios cannot be improved.

4.12 Having plotted the ratios for products, markets and product/market cells on the three grids we can see at a glance how each of the firm's products is performing in each of the markets supplied. We can see which are "stars" performing better than average and therefore where we should be looking to increase sales. We can see which are the "cash cows" which need careful attention as they pass through the production process to ensure that costs do not exceed estimates. We can identify the "question marks" where we need to decide whether they have sufficient potential to warrant investment in equipment that will enable a larger proportion of the work to be done in house. Finally we can identify the "dogs", which, unless some dramatic improvement can be achieved, we should

Illustration 23 Product/markets ranked as "Cash cows", "Stars", "Question marks" and "Dogs"

Markets	Products	Sales	VA/S%	VA:W	C/S% £	C/VA%
"Cash cows"						
Motor	Manuals	30000	65.0%	4.33	50.0%	76.9%
Motor	Brochures	400000	67.5%	3.38	47.5%	70.4%
Engineering	Leaflets	145000	69.0%	3.33	48.3%	70.0%
Engineering	Brochures	250000	68.0%	3.09	46.0%	67.6%
"Stars"						
Pharmaceuticals	Labels	375000	72.0%	7.50	62.4%	86.7%
Motor	Leaflets	165000	76.7%	6.66	65.2%	85.0%
Motor	Posters	85000	71.8%	6.42	60.6%	84.4%
Financial	Greetings	175000	71.4%	6.25	60.0%	84.0%
Computers	Manuals	85750	76.7%	5.98	63.8%	83.3%
Computers	Labels	150000	71.3%	5.94	59.3%	83.2%
Financial	Brochures	303750	73.7%	5.59	60.5%	82.1%
Engineering	Manuals	115500	74.0%	5.52	60.6%	81.9%
"Question marks"						
Pharmaceuticals	Leaflets	310000	61.3%	7.04	52.6%	85.8%
Travel	Posters	210000	54.8%	6.57	46.4%	84.8%
Giftware	Greetings	120000	56.7%	6.48	47.9%	84.6%
Travel	Brochures	275000	56.4%	6.46	47.6%	84.5%
Giftware	Posters	85000	45.3%	6.42	38.2%	84.4%
Giftware	Labels	90000	50.0%	5.49	40.9%	81.8%
Travel	Catalogues	180000	52.8%	5.28	42.8%	81.1%
Travel	Labels	75000	49.3%	4.93	39.3%	79.7%
"Dogs"						
Textiles	Catalogues	700000	57.1%	3.15	39.0%	68.3%
Public bodies	Labels	70000	47.1%	3.00	31.4%	66.7%
Office	Labels	70000	52.9%	2.89	34.6%	65.4%
Office	Greetings	125000	55.2%	2.88	36.0%	65.2%
Public bodies	Leaflets	220000	43.0%	2.86	28.0%	65.1%
Textiles	Labels	190000	52.1%	2.83	33.7%	64.6%

be looking to substituting. We now have a sound base on which to start building a marketing strategy.

4.13 In addition to plotting the performance ratios in this way on a contribution contour grid, or as an alternative, it should be possible to programme an information system to sort and rank the product/market cell data derived from the job sheets so as to produce lists of "cash cows", "stars" etc, by defining the four categories as follows;

	VA/S	VA:W
"Cash cows"	>62.0%	<4.43
"Stars"	>62.0%	>4.43
"Question marks"	<62.0%	>4.43
"Dogs"	<62.0%	<4.43

The lists can then be ranked by value added:wages.

CHAPTER 5

DEVELOPING A MARKETING STRATEGY

- Changing the mix of work

5.01 Having located products, markets and product/market cells on the contribution contour grid, we can now start to examine each in turn in the context of the information which the firm has about each market, the collection of which has been described in chapter 2. This is the first step in developing a marketing strategy to improve performance. The aims should be to:

- direct the sales effort towards increasing sales of the "stars", the products/markets in the top right hand segment;

- take action internally to improve the efficiency with which the firm produces the "cash cows", the products in the top left hand segment;

- look towards developing in house production facilities for the "question marks", the products in the bottom right segment; and

- begin to substitute the "dogs", the products in the bottom left hand segment; but do not simply off load the latter, without putting something in their place.

5.02 By changing the mix of work in this way management can start to improve the overall performance of the firm. Relatively small shifts will produce significant improvements. The products in the top right hand segment, the "stars", are the jobs that are doing pretty well overall, need to be developed further and allow scope for development. There is cash to spare, price can be used as a marketing tool because value added:wages performance is better than average. Money can be spent to boost the selling effort. Even if the value added:wages were to fall slightly from say 6 to 5.5 in this illustration it would still be much better than the average of 4.43.

5.03 Management needs to be pulling in all the information it has assembled in the market segmentation exercise in chapter 2 to enable it to identify whether and where sales can be increased. This could mean simply selling more to existing customers, but the company might already be their major supplier and unlikely to gain a larger share of their custom. It could mean selling to other customers in the same market, i.e. increasing market share. Or it could mean looking for similar markets where the product might be needed. The high value added:wages ratio allows for "price leverage" to open up new markets and/or customers. At the same time, thinking back to the break even chart and the definition of price as the value per unit of volume or utilisation, it can be seen that because the value added:wages ratio is higher than average the firm will actually be *achieving a price increase.* It will be generating additional revenue through a price increase rather than through a volume increase.

5.04 Jobs in the top left hand segment, the "cash cows" tend to be fairly high volume relatively low profit work. The value added/sales ratio is above average but the value added:wages ratio is below average. There is therefore no scope for trying to increase sales by price reductions. If sales are to be increased in this area action will be required to improve production methods so as to improve the value added:wages ratio. Orders which require overtime working should be resisted as they will have a disastrous effect on the value added:wages ratio. The likely impact of an increase in sales in this area will be a need to increase utilisation. In other words, thinking back to the break even chart, increased revenue generation will be the result of increased volume. There are limits in terms of utilisation efficiency to the size of such a volume increase.

5.05 Products in the bottom right hand segment, the "question marks" are often jobs where the firm is attempting to enter a new market-place but is not yet sure of the amount of resources it should devote to it or whether the market will take off. Quite a lot of outwork is bought in. Further commercial appraisal is required to see whether it is worth investing in production facilities.

5.06 Products in the bottom left hand segment, the "dogs", are the ones which are detracting from the overall performance of the company because they are below average both in terms of their value added/sales ratio and their value added:wages ratio. This work needs to be looked at very carefully to see whether there is any scope for improvement. If there is not, management should be looking to replace this work with other higher performance work. But management should not under any circumstances start disposing of the work without putting something in its place. It is still generating value added even though the ratios are below average. Remember there is some 50% underutilisation - "work" which is generating no added value whatsoever and eating into contribution. So work which is at least bringing in some contribution should not be given up without being replaced by work giving a higher contribution. But this work needs to be managed with great care to make sure it goes through the plant as efficiently as possible.

5.07 It has to be accepted that in an industry such as printing where much of the work is bespoke and the input therefore random and determined by the customer it is unlikely that utilisation will exceed 60-70%. Operational research has established that where there is random input, queueing problems start to occur above 60/65% utilisation. Delays start to creep into the system, overtime has to be worked and customers become dissatisfied. In the printing industry variations in demand are accommodated by having excess capacity in either machinery or manpower or both.

- Directing sales personnel

5.08 Having targeted markets, management can now start to direct the sales personnel's efforts more precisely to those markets and customers where the firm wants to expand sales of those products which are producing the best performance in terms of value added/sales and value added:wages ratios. Instead of just bringing in any work which they can get irrespective of its impact on the overall performance of the firm, sales personnel can now be directed to go for high performance work. Furthermore, with the help of the contribution grid and the methodology to be outlined in the next chapter, they can also be armed with pricing information that will enable them to quote a price that the market will bear but which will also meet the firm's criteria for performance.

CHAPTER 6

USING PRICE TO SUPPORT THE MARKETING STRATEGY

- Organisational implications of pricing

6.01 Pricing is a difficult area. Previous paragraphs have demonstrated that pricing is a vital ingredient within the profit equation. In some cases price alone is used by some companies as a means of attracting work, with all the attendant risks. On the other hand research has shown that differential pricing, based on market segmentation which recognises the differences between the various product/markets, can be very successful.

6.02 However, the introduction of a pro-active pricing policy requires a significant change of attitude in most companies. While it would be wrong to suggest that all the successful companies are wholly committed to marginal pricing, it is likely that most are using the principles of market pricing. A major spin-off for companies doing this is that they became very knowledgeable about the market and develop a keen awareness of the prevailing conditions.

- Using price as a lever to open up markets

6.03 In chapter 5 it was demonstrated that jobs done for product/market cells in the "stars" segment of the contribution contour grid offered scope for using price as a lever to increase sales to and shares of those markets. By definition such jobs are generating higher than average value added:wages ratios. To make practical use of this knowledge we first need to establish what prices those

77

markets will bear. We then need to have a method of pricing that will make use of this information and also tell us the levels of value added and contribution and the performance ratios that particular prices will generate. We can use the information provided by the value added and contribution analysis of job sheets. The means of doing so are now built into management information systems. Here we explain the methodology and the pricing decision making process.

- How to calculate pricing options

6.04 Whereas in the value added and contribution analysis of job sheets we started with the price received from the customer and then deducted the costs to arrive at value added and contribution, here we start with the various costs and build towards a price. Illustration 24 sets out a marketing pricing cost sheet to be used and paragraphs 6.05 to 6.09 explain how to use it.

6.05 When a potential job comes in for an estimate fill in the information on the estimating sheet as follows. First, identify the job in terms of the type of product and the market the customer is in. Second, enter the cost of any materials required and any outwork and sum them to reach a figure for purchases. Third, estimate the time that the job will take within each department and multiply by the "hourly wage only rate" for the respective departments, which will have already been calculated for the value added analysis of job sheets, and then sum the wage costs. Fourth, extract from the previous value added analysis of job sheets the three performance ratios for the relevant product/market cell to which this particular job has been allocated and use them to calculate three price options as explained below. Each will reflect what has been achieved in terms of price and performance ratios in previous sales of that particular product to that market.

- Productivity price

6.06 The productivity price is calculated by multiplying the estimated wage costs (£762.96) by the value added:wages ratio (6.46) and adding on the cost of purchases (£3525). The price reflects what has previously been achieved in the sense that the value added:wages ratio used was the average that has been generated in previous sales so that particular product/market cell, i.e. £6.46 per £ of wages.

Illustration 24 Market pricing cost sheet

JOB NUMBER	1	CUSTOMER CODE	JBLOGGS
PRODUCT CODE	LEAFLETS	MARKET CODE	TRAVEL

Purchases			£
Materials			3000
Outwork			
Agents			150
Prepress			
Press			
Finishing			350
Transport			25
Total outwork			525
Total Purchases (P)			3525

Wage costs	Hours	Hrly. wage only rate	Wage cost
Pre-press	40	15.00	600.00
Press	12	13.58	162.96
Finishing		11.00	0
Total wage costs (W)			762.96

Ratios for product/market cell Leaflets/Travel
    VAS = 56/4% VA:W = 6.46 C/S = 47.6%

Illustration 24 Market pricing cost sheet (continued)

Pricing options

Productivity price (P1) = W x (VA:W) + M	8453.72
Materials price (P2) = M x 100/[100-(VA/S)]	8084.86
Contribution price (P3) = (M+W) x 100/[100-(C/S)]	8183.13

	P1	P2	P3
Price	8453.72	8084.86	8183.13
Purchases	3525.00	3525.00	3525.00
Value added	4928.72	4559.86	4658.13
Wage costs	762.96	762.96	762.96
Contribution	4165.76	3796.90	3895.17

Performance ratios

VA/S	58.3%	56.4%	56.9%
VA:W	6.46	5.98	6.11
C/S	49.3%	47.0%	47.6%
C/VA	84.5%	83.3%	83.6%

- Materials price

6.07 The materials price is calculated by multiplying the cost of purchases (£3525) by 100 and dividing by 100 minus the value added/sales ratio (56.4). In other words the cost of purchases has been grossed up so that the price less the cost of purchases i.e. the value added when divided by the price would equal the appropriate ratio. This likewise reflects the market price in that on average on previous jobs for this product/market cell a value added/ sales ratio of 56.4% has been generated.

- Contribution price

6.08 The contribution price is calculated by adding the cost of purchases (£3525) and the wage costs (£762.96), multiplying by 100 and then dividing by 100 minus the contribution/sales ratio (47.6).

6.09 The three prices can then be entered in the table along with the other costs so that value added, contribution and the performance ratios can be calculated for each of them.

- Choosing the right pricing option

6.10 We now have a range of prices with either the productivity price or the materials price as the highest depending on whether purchases or wages costs are the higher, and with the contribution price always the middle one. All three prices reflect what has previously been achieved in that particular product/market cell and can therefore justifiably be referred to as "market based prices".

6.11 The choice of price will depend on a number of factors related on the one hand to the market situation and the firm's objectives in that market, and on the other hand to the situation within the firm, the level of utilisation, and the state of the order book.

6.12 The best price to go for is the contribution price, which is in the middle of the range. However, if you are well placed in the market and have a unique selling point or if order books are full then you could well pitch for the highest price. On the other hand if the firm is short of work or trying to establish itself in a new market then it should be prepared to go down to the lower price. The actual price finally quoted does not necessarily have to be within the range. The point of calculating prices in this way is that it is possible very quickly and easily to see the impact of whatever price is quoted on value added, and the performance ratios. Management information and pricing systems using the value added analysis approach will automatically provide this information for pricing a job.

- Providing sales personnel with a price and the discretion to negotiate.

6.13 Using this approach it is possible to allow sales personnel scope for negotiation. They need not simply be given a quote and have to say "take it or leave it". They can be given a range within which to negotiate, with a floor price below which they must not go, and above which they can be told to obtain the best price commensurate with securing the job.

CHAPTER 7

DEVELOPING A BUSINESS PLAN

- Using value added and contribution analysis to develop a business plan

7.01 We can now draw together the various strands of the value added approach to profit by making the best use of a management information system and look at how it can be used to develop a business plan. For this we need to return to the analysis of the management accounts. The analysis of the previous year's accounts started with sales and worked through to value added, contribution and finally the bottom line of net profit. To develop a business plan we start at the bottom line with a profit objective and work our way upwards calculating at each stage how much contribution, value added and, finally, sales need to be generated to produce that level of profit.

7.02 We set out a very simple business plan with the new profit objective in illustration 25. We start from the bottom with the new profit objective of £450,000 a 50% increase on the profit in the previous year. To this we add overheads which we assume will increase to £1,500,000. The contribution that is needed therefore will be £1,950,000. To this we add wage costs which we assume will also increase to £1,500,000. This leaves us needing to generate £3,450,000 of value added. If we assume that the raw material and outwork purchases required will be the same proportion of final sales as before i.e. 38%, then to calculate the sales which need to be generated, value added has to be grossed up accordingly by 100/62. This works out at sales of £5,565,000. Thus in order to generate a 50% increase in profits and cope with overhead and wage cost increases of 7.1% sales will need to be increased by 13.9%.

Illustration 25 Constructing a business plan

	£'000
= Sales	5565
+ Purchases	2115
= Value added	3450
+ Direct wages	1500
= Contribution	1950
+ Overheads	1500
Net Profit	450

7.03 The overall performance ratios would be as follows:

Illustration 26 Business plan overall performance ratios

Value added/sales	62.0%
Value added:wages	2.30
Contribution/sales	35.0%
Contribution/value added	56.5%
Net profit/sales	8.1%

7.04 The significant change in the ratios from the previous year is the increase in value added:wages from 2.21 to 2.30. This means that the firm will need to be looking for jobs that bring in a higher value added:wages ratio.

7.05 Management can now begin to develop the marketing strategy to support the business plan. They know what sales will need to be and they know the overall value added:wages ratio that needs to be generated (2.30). Assuming that utilisation will be 50% they will know that the value added:wages ratio on the jobs done will need to average 4.60 (2.30/50x100). Anything lower than this and utilisation will need to be higher to compensate.

7.06 They can now draw up a sales budget using all the information put together during the market segmentation exercise alongside the value added and contribution analysis of the job sheets which identified and ranked the various products, markets and product/market cells in terms of their performance ratios. The basic aim is to target those product/market cells which generate the best performance ratios, the "stars". The assessment of what can be achieved must be realistic otherwise spurious figures can get into the plans and the exercise will become misleading and meaningless.

7.07 When the forecasts for the different markets have been made the projected sales figures and the performance ratios can be put into the computer and aggregated to see whether the necessary value added and contribution will be generated. The chances of this coming out right the first time are slim and some further adjustments are likely to be necessary and the figures reworked until a consistent and coherent plan has been drawn up.

7.08 All that remains is for the plan to be put into practice. The sales force can be targeted and promotional work can be undertaken in those markets which are going to provide the best returns. With the knowledge of the performance ratios that are required quotations can be geared to achieving them using the new method of pricing.

Illustration 27 Revised marketing budget changing the balance of products and markets

	Sales £	Purchases £	Value added £	Wages £	Contribution £	VA/S	VA:W	C/S	C/VA
Computers	255000	68144	186856	31368	155488	73.3%	5.96	61.0%	83.2%
Engineering	510000	154848	355152	100402	254750	69.6%	3.54	50.0%	71.7%
Financial	630000	171070	458930	78956	379974	72.8%	5.81	60.3%	82.8%
Giftware	390000	189712	200288	32654	167634	51.4%	6.13	43.0%	83.7%
Motor	680000	203000	477000	113000	364000	70.1%	4.22	53.5%	76.3%
Office	180000	82154	97846	33969	63877	54.4%	2.88	35.5%	65.3%
Pharmaceuticals	785000	258092	526908	72163	454745	67.1%	7.30	57.9%	86.3%
Public bodies	270000	151293	118707	39041	79666	44.0%	3.04	29.5%	67.1%
Textiles	870000	382213	487787	158360	329427	56.1%	3.08	37.9%	67.5%
Travel	995000	454473	540527	90088	450439	54.3%	6.00	45.3%	83.3%
Total sales	556500	2115000	3450000	750000	2700000	62.0%	4.60	48.5%	78.3%

7.09 Most important a constant check can be kept on progress to see whether targets are being met and the performance ratios are being achieved at the right level of utilisation. Where they are not, adjustments can be made and efforts increased or redirected.

- Planning and the use of computers

7.10 The printing industry is changing apace and competition from home and overseas is ever increasing. Never has it been more important for managers to fully understand the nature and make up of the business they are getting and seeking. It is particularly important to be able to put some direction into marketing in order to stop being busy fools.

7.11 The procedures and calculations described in the previous chapters set out to give managers the information they need to make informed decisions. It gives information about markets as well as giving good, objective, financial information about prices which will ensure that the company improves the chances of obtaining work whilst, at the same time, getting as high a price as possible within the prevailing competitive conditions.

7.12 The volume of work involved in doing the work described would be totally counter-productive if it were to be done manually. It would require systematic examination of sales ledgers and cost sheets for every estimate and completed job and this would require an army of numerate and accurate clerks. In the process the customer would find another supplier whilst waiting for a quote.

7.13 The invention of the micro computer however has made the procedures described completely within the scope of all printing companies and many software houses offer systems which take the value added approach. Such systems are able to offer substantial memory for storage of the history of products and markets, high speed calculation so that the different scenarios can be identified quickly and above all accuracy and repeatability so that the same answers are given irrespective of the user. However this does assume that the information which is used by the computer is consistent and accurate.

7.14 The introduction of a system of this nature will however require not just the purchase of a computer and software but a change in the manner the business is managed. The requirement will be for an outward, marketing led approach which may require a shift of emphasis for cost to revenue management. Only then will the company be able to get "value added" from the installation of a computerised management information system and put profit on the bottom line.

APPENDIX A

VALUE ADDED AND CONTRIBUTION ANALYSIS OF MANAGEMENT ACCOUNTS

	£'000
Sales	5050
Discounts	50
Total Sales (S)	5000
Purchases	
Materials	1500
Outwork	400
Total Purchases (P)	1900
Value added (VA) = S-P	3100
Direct Wages (W)	1400
Contribution (C) =VA-W	1700
Overheads	
Admin. salaries	570
Rent and rates	150
Light, heat power	50
Transport	40
Travel, entertainment	60
Insurance	30
Telephone	20
Maintenance	75
Consumables	80
Professional fees	10
Advertising	10
Training, recruitment	20
Trade indemnity	20

Stationery	20
Bad debts	15
Total Overheads	1170
Profit before Depr., Interest, and Tax	530
Depreciation, leasing	180
Interest	50
PROFIT BEFORE TAX	300

REFERENCES

Accounting Standards Steering Committee
The Corporate Report
July 1975

Chapman D. J.
Measures For Success
NEDO Books 1984

Parker R. H.
Understanding company financial statements
Penguin Business—1988

Printing Industry Sector Working Party
Make Ready for Success
NEDO Books 1981

Winkler J.
Pricing For Results
Heineman 1989